In the Jungle

Written by Becca Heddle

This is the jungle.

Parrots fly in the jungle.

Monkeys swing in the jungle.

Flowers bloom in the jungle.

9

Big cats hunt in the jungle.

We live in the jungle!

13

We live here!

Ideas for reading

Written by Clare Dowdall, PhD
Lecturer and Primary Literacy Consultant

Learning objectives: children read and understand simple sentences; children know about similarities and differences in relation to places, objects, materials and living things; they talk about how environments might vary from one another; they know about similarities and differences between themselves and others, and among families, communities and traditions

Curriculum links: Understanding of the world: The world

High frequency words: in, the, this, is, we

Interest words: jungle, parrots, fly, monkeys, swing, flowers, bloom, hunt

Resources: ICT, sticky notes, paper and coloured pencils for drawing

Word count: 30

Getting started

- Ask children to close their eyes and imagine that they are in a jungle. Ask one child at a time to describe what he or she can see, hear, feel and smell.

- Look at the front and back cover. Discuss what children can see in the images and compare this to their imagined jungles.

- Read the title and blurb aloud. Model how to decode and pronounce the word *jungle*. Discuss any tricky words that the children do not recognise, e.g. *what's*, and help them to practise reading the blurb fluently.

Reading and responding

- Turn to pp2–3. Read the text aloud together. Ask children to predict which creatures may live at the top and at the bottom of the jungle.

- Turn to pp4–5. Ask children to practise reading the longer word *parrots*. Discuss what children know about parrots.

- Ask children to continue reading to the end of the book, supporting and praising them as they read.